PRICK UP YOUR EARS

T0353306

Simon Bent

PRICK UP YOUR EARS

inspired by John Lahr's biography and
the diaries of Joe Orton

OBERON BOOKS
LONDON

First published in 2009 by Oberon Books Ltd
521 Caledonian Road, London N7 9RH
Tel: 020 7607 3637 / Fax: 020 7607 3629
e-mail: info@oberonbooks.com
www.oberonbooks.com

A catalogue record for this book is available from the British
Library.

ISBN: 978-1-84002-945-1

Cover design by Dewynters, London
Photograph by Simon Turtle

Characters (in order of appearance)

KENNETH HALLIWELL
JOE ORTON
MRS CORDEN

The action of the play takes place in the one bedroom flat shared by Joe Orton and Kenneth Halliwell at twenty-five Noel Rd, Islington, London. In it are two beds, a writing desk with a chair and a typewriter on it. The kitchen and bathroom are offstage.

During the play a collage, made of pictures taken from books, magazines and newspapers grows and spreads across the walls of the flat: a riotous confusion of conflicting and disturbing images, the sprawl of Kenneth Halliwell's subconscious at work. By the end of the play it should feel as if the room can hardly contain the collage, that it is about to burst at the seams under the weight of its intensity.

Prick Up Your Ears was first performed at Richmond Theatre, London, on 26 August 2009 with the following cast:

KEN, Matt Lucas
JOE, Chris New
MRS CORDEN, Gwen Taylor

Director Daniel Kramer
Designer Peter McKintosh
Lighting Designer Peter Mumford
Sound Designer Gareth Owen for Orbital

The production subsequently toured and opened at the Comedy Theatre, London, on 17 September 2009. It was produced by Sonia Friedman Productions, Kim Poster for Stanhope Productions and Lee Menzies in association with Sean Sweeney.

The printed text may differ slightly from the play as performed.

Act One

KEN in pyjamas
Sitting up in bed
Writing furiously

Withdraws pencil
Chews pencil
Studies notebook in agony

KEN: No.

Flamboyantly crosses out what he's written
Puts pencil to paper

Yes.

Writes furiously, laughing much at what he's writing
Withdraws pencil
Chews pencil
Studies notebook in agony

Got it.

Puts pencil to paper
Writes some more furiously

Arrrrrrrrrrrrgh.

Throws down pencil and notebook in exhaustion
Lies down on bed writhing clutching his head in pain and groaning
Suddenly stops

And my castaway today needs no introduction, regarded by many as a true renaissance man – he bestrides the arts, a literary and artistic colossuss – novelist, playwright, poet – his early novels although at first neglected are now considered modern classics, these include such masterpieces as, *The Silver Bucket, The Mechanical Womb, The Last Days of Sodom, The Boy Hairdresser,*

> *Picks up notebook*

and his most recent triumph, (*Reads.*) *Priapus in the Shrubbery* – I am of course talking about Sir Kenneth Halliwell. Welcome to your desert island Kenneth, 'Thank you, Roy'. Ken, you don't mind me calling you Ken, 'No, no, not at all, Roy'. It's hard to believe now but for years you went unrecognised and languished in poverty – tell me, what kept you going through all those early days of rejection. 'Talent, Roy, sheer bloody talent'. So, your first desert island disc –

> *Gets up and takes out record from sleeve*

"The Overture' from *Pal Joey*'

> *Puts it on record player*

Because it reminds me of those early days – when I shared a one room flat with struggling writer John Orton, at twenty-five Noel Road, Islington.

> *Turns on record player*
> *Music plays: 'Overture', Pal Joey*
> *KEN lies on bed*
> *And closes eyes*

> *Enter JOE*
> *Donkey jacket and cap*
> *Army surplus canvas shoulder bag*
> *With bag of shopping*

> *JOE turns off music*

JOE: What are you doing.

KEN: Working.

> *JOE crosses to desk and dumps shoulder bag*

JOE: You're not working.

KEN: I do some of my best work lying down.

JOE: Time to get up. Embrace the day.

KEN: Do I have to.

JOE: Yes. You haven't been out for two days.

KEN: You've been for a walk.

JOE: Along the canal.

>*JOE exits with bag of shopping into kitchen*

KEN: Up to no good on the towpath, no wonder you're happy.

>*JOE re-enters from kitchen*

JOE: Up, there's work to do.

KEN: I'm dying.

JOE: Have you eaten.

KEN: I managed a cheese sandwich.

JOE: You should try going out.

KEN: I can't.

JOE: Get out, go for a bicycle ride.

KEN: I'm dying.

JOE: You're not dying.

KEN: A long slow malingering death.

JOE: There's nothing like a good bike ride to blow away the cobwebs.

>*JOE takes off coat*

KEN: On a bike you're vulnerable to assassination.

JOE: You do, you need to get out.

KEN: A moving target. How was the library.

JOE: Empty. But for Ahmed the Egyptian reading the papers.

KEN: You like Ahmed the Egptian.

JOE: You like Ahmed the Egyptian.

KEN: Full of Eastern promise.

JOE: Lunchbox the size of an anaconda. I know what you want.

KEN: Then give it me.

JOE: Go out and get it.

KEN: Tell me.

JOE: No.

KEN: Please.

JOE: Beg.

KEN: No, please don't make me beg.

JOE: Beg.

KEN: Please.

JOE: More.

KEN: I'm begging.

JOE: What do you want.

KEN: You know what I want.

JOE: Tell me.

KEN: I have to.

JOE: Yes.

KEN: No.

JOE: Tell me.

KEN: I can't.

JOE: You have to.

KEN: That's right, make me, make me say it.

JOE: Tell me.

KEN: It's big.

JOE: What's big.

KEN: Ahmed, Ahmed the Egyptian.

JOE: Now get dressed.

KEN: Oh, you're no fun.

JOE: You're no fun.

> *KEN takes off his pyjama top and puts on his shirt*

KEN: Kenneth *contra mundum.*

> *KEN starts to button his shirt*

> *JOE takes two library books out of canvas shoulder bag*

JOE: I could've stolen every book they've got and nobody would have noticed.

KEN: It's not stealing.

JOE: What do you call taking library books without permission.

KEN: We put them back.

JOE: Only after we've written in them.

KEN: We don't disturb the novel, never the actual book, only it's fly leaf and cover.

JOE: Urban guerilla warfare.

KEN: So skilfully done it's hardly perceptible. And our list doesn't just include fiction.

JOE: Horticulture and gardening.

KEN: Historical tomes.

JOE: Some of the nation's most treasured poets. I've seen readers complain when a book hasn't lived up to one of our doctored covers.

KEN: It's a form of literary criticism.

JOE: It's the only way we can get into print.

KEN: Thus far. Let me see, what did you get.

> *JOE picks up books and hands one to KEN*

> *Clouds of Witness*, by Dorothy L Sayers.

JOE: You like whodunits.

KEN: I do.

> *KEN drops book*
> *Holds out his hand*
> *JOE gives him the other book*

Oh, thank you very much.
Masterpieces of the Renaissance.

JOE: Some pictures for our book covers.

KEN: I feel my muse. Strike while the iron's hot.

> *KEN kicks Dorothy Sayers across the floor in the direction of the typewriter*
> *JOE picks it up and takes off dust jacket*

Places.

> *JOE to typewriter and threads dust jacket into it – KEN to 'stage' and prepares to extemporise*

KEN: *Clouds of Witness* – by Dorothy Sayers with additional cover notes by Professor Kenneth Halliwell and his amanuensis Joe Orton – ready?

JOE: Ready.

As KEN extemporises he paces up and down growing in excitement and grandiloquence

KEN: When little Betty Macdree says that she has been interfered with her mother takes her to the police station and to everyone's surprise the little girl identifies PC Brenda Coolidge as her attacker.

JOE: Hang on, hang on.

KEN: Keep up, keep up, I'm in the flow – don't and I'll trade you in for a younger sexier model.

JOE: There.

KEN: A search is made of the women's police barracks. What is found there is a seven inch phallus and a pair of knickers of the kind used by Betty.

JOE: Oh, yes.

KEN: Yes. This is one of the most enthralling stories ever written by Miss Sayers.

JOE: I'll say.

KEN: It is the only one in which the murder weapon is concealed not for reasons of fear, but for reasons of decency.

He stands and waits as JOE quickly finishes up typing

Well?

JOE: Yes, it's good, but there's something missing.

JOE types

KEN: Did they say that about *Crime and Punishment* when it was first published? *War and Peace, Pride and Prejudice, Moby Dick.*

JOE gives dust jacket to KEN to read:

(*Reads.*) 'Read this behind closed doors. And have a good shit while you are reading.'

JOE: Well?

KEN: Maybe a little crude towards the end.

JOE: The trouble with your writing is that you refuse to pack a punch, you don't know what you want –

KEN: And you do.

JOE: Yes – get educated, get published, get famous.

KEN: And so we will – I've arranged a meeting with a small but reputable publishing house at the Imperial Hotel, Russell Square, in the Beaufort Bar.

JOE: When.

KEN: Tonight.

JOE: I've got an appointment with a gentleman in a toilet on the Holloway Road.

KEN: Cancel it.

JOE: I can't – there are too many variables.

KEN: Such as?

JOE: The gentleman's identity and exact time of our rendezvous remain as yet unknown.

KEN: You've made no formal arrangement.

JOE: It's deliberately kept that way so as to avoid disappointment.

KEN: There's nothing definite about it.

JOE: Oh it's quite definite. He doesn't know that I'm coming but I know that I am going. He does not know who I am and I do not know who he is, but we each expect the other.

KEN: I won't be stood up for a complete stranger. We're going to the Imperial Hotel, Russell Square. Prepare to be published.

JOE: It's best not to get up your hopes.

KEN: Faith, have faith.

JOE: I'm an atheist.

KEN: Faith, a necessary prerequisite for any artist – belief in oneself.

JOE: What's the difference between that and delusion.

KEN: Doubt, the enemy of hope. We must make the right impression.

    Takes off pyjama bottoms

Fetch me my best trousers.

JOE: You can go on your own.

KEN: After all I've done for you. We must make a good impression, fetch me my best trousers.

JOE: They won't fit. You haven't worn them since Coronation Day.

KEN: They've shrunk.

JOE: No.

KEN: What are you suggesting.

JOE: Nothing.

    Alarm clock goes off

KEN: Ah – it's time for our programme. Turn on the wireless.

JOE: (*Turns off alarm clock.*) It's that time already.

KEN: Turn it on, it's time.

    JOE turns on wireless

No, wait, wait – where's the pinny, I need the pinny, get me the pinny.

JOE rushes into the kitchen

Coconut shells.

KEN takes out a pair of coconut shells from under his bed

Hurry up John or I'll start without you, another exciting instalment in the daily life of ordinary middle class folk at Vagina Lodge in the county of Muddlesex –

Enter JOE with pinny and tray of props
Cup, saucer, newspaper, etc.
For making sound effects

JOE gives KEN the pinny
KEN puts the pinny on
JOE 'stands by' ready with the tape recorder

One day these recordings will come to be seen as the Dead Sea scrolls of radio broadcasting.

JOE: Ready?

KEN: Ready.

TOGETHER: Five – four – three – two –

JOE turns on tape recorder

On the wireless the introduction music to Mrs Dale's Diary

WIRELESS: *Mrs Dale's Diary*, a recording of the daily happenings in the life of a doctor's wife.

JOE switches wireless off

JOE: (*Whispers.*) Action!

KEN: (*As Mrs Dale.*) Well, what a weekend it has been, very surprising indeed. It all began on Saturday morning while I was idly massaging myself and reached under the bed for the jar of Vaseline and found it missing. It wasn't until we were sitting down to breakfast that I said anything.

For the following dialogue MRS DALE and MOTHER are played by KEN, and SALLY and JIM are played by JOE

MRS DALE: Jim, darling.

KEN indicates to JOE to rattle cup and saucer
Then to stop

JIM: Yes, Mary my dear.

MRS DALE: Have you been using my Vaseline.

JIM: What on earth for, Mary, dear.

MRS DALE: Oh, I don't know, it's gone missing.

JIM: Perhaps Mother-in-law's had it. Oh, here she comes.

KEN makes the sound of a creaking door opening
JOE makes the sound of it shutting and the footsteps of MOTHER's
entry

Let's ask her.

MOTHER: Ask who and what you horrid little man.

JIM: There's nothing little about me Mother-in-law.

MOTHER: I know, you've got such a big head, and most of the boys in the village have seen it.

JIM: Mother-in-law, a jar of Vaseline from under our bed has gone missing.

MOTHER: What on earth would I want with such a thing.

JIM: Who knows, Mother-in-law.

MRS DALE: It's certainly a mystery my dear and that's for sure. (*Whispers.*) Coconuts.

JOE picks up coconut shells and gallops with them

Look, here comes Sally galloping towards Vagina Lodge on her new black Arab stallion Ram-Rod.

SALLY: Whoa boy whoa.

JOE rears like a horse shrieking

Steady Ram-Rod steady.

JOE canters and stops

MOTHER: Quick bolt the door, don't let her in, tell her to keep that horse away from me – the last time he smelt Captain on me and he tried to mount me from behind.

SALLY: You led him on Mother.

MOTHER: I most certainly did not, Sally.

SALLY: You kept stroking his balls and feeding him sugar lumps, Mother.

MOTHER: Lies, lies and more lies, Sally. I'm not staying here to be insulted, Sally.

Sound of MOTHER exiting and door slamming shut

JIM: Oh, dear now look what you've done.

MRS DALE: Never mind.

SALLY: So, what's the news with you, do tell.

MRS DALE: The Vaseline from under our bed's gone missing.

SALLY: Stolen.

MRS DALE: We don't know yet not for sure, it could be anywhere.

SALLY: Well when did you last use it.

MRS DALE: When the Allies entered Paris, we celebrated – I let Jim lubricate the back door and use it as an entrance.

Knock at door

Who's that knocking at the door now?

JIM: I don't know dear, but it's not me.

MRS DALE: And it's not me.

Knocking at door

JIM: Then who on earth can it be.

MRS CORDEN: (*Off.*) John, Kenneth.

JOE: Mrs Corden, what does she want.

KEN: Ignore it. She'll go away

JOE: No, she won't.

MRS CORDEN: (*Off.*) Is anyone there.

Knock at door

(*Off.*) It's only me.

JOE: (*Shouts.*) Come in, Mrs Corden.

KEN switches off tape recorder

Enter MRS CORDEN

MRS CORDEN: Oh, there you are.

KEN: Yes, here we are.

MRS CORDEN: I was hoping you'd be out.

KEN: Sorry to disappoint.

MRS CORDEN: I'm not interrupting anything, am I?

JOE: No, no not at all.

JOE picks up tray of sound effects and exits into the kitchen with it

MRS CORDEN: Kenneth, you've got no trousers on.

KEN: No, no, that's right, no trousers, I'm giving my legs some air.

MRS CORDEN: And you're wearing a pinafore.

KEN: Yes, quite, we are merely improvising, honing the tools of our trade. We are don't you know both classically trained actors, fellow graduates of the Royal Academy of Dramatic Art and as such it's important that we stretch our wings every now and again.

MRS CORDEN: I wouldn't normally intrude –

JOE re-enters from kitchen

KEN: You're not intruding.

JOE: Ken was very good at mime.

KEN: I like to keep my hand in.

JOE: It's only when he opens his mouth onstage that he comes unstuck.

MRS CORDEN: You know I don't like to intrude, you're grown men entitled to your privacy, but there are two suspicious looking gentlemen at the front door claiming to be police officers and asking for you by name.

KEN: What do they want with us?

MRS CORDEN: At first I thought it was the Gas Board –

JOE: What makes you think they're police.

MRS CORDEN: Only the police would feel free to knock on a perfect stranger's door any time they choose.

JOE: They think they can get away with murder.

KEN: They do get away with murder.

MRS CORDEN: The moment they said who they were I felt guilty.

KEN: What do they want.

JOE: We're just two innocent lads with natural inclinations larking around.

KEN: Boys will be boys, the judiciary understand.

JOE: Some of my most cherished moments involve going before a judge.

MRS CORDEN: They're investigating the unauthorised disappearance of some books from the shelves of a local library.

KEN: Oh.

MRS CORDEN: They wanted to barge right in, but I told them this isn't Russia we're living in, not yet – don't they have anything better to waste the taxpayers money on, don't they read the papers, don't they know this city is crawling with muggers, rapists and foreign nationals that it's not safe for a woman my age to walk the streets at night.

JOE: Who'd steal a library book, when they're already free. It'd be like paying your wife for sex.

KEN: I don't have a wife.

JOE: Surely they can't arrest us for that.

MRS CORDEN: I told them you're both writers, respectable gentlemen with plenty of books of your own, I told them they won't find any library books in my flat – I won't have them in the house, you never know where they've been. What do you want me to do, shall I say you're not in.

KEN: No send them up immediately Mrs Corden, we have nothing to fear from the long arm of the law, this is England and we have the finest criminal injustice system in the world.

MRS CORDEN: They want you to go down. What shall I tell them.

KEN picks up his trousers

KEN: *Festina Lente –*

Shakes out trousers

Celerity contempered with cunctation.

JOE: She can't say that, she'll get arrested.

KEN: Tell them I'm putting on my trousers, I will be down shortly.

JOE: I thought you couldn't go out.

KEN: I've never been able to refuse a man in uniform.

KEN pulls on his trousers

MRS CORDEN: That's right Kenneth you put your trousers on – Mr Corden always feels more able with his trousers on. I'm sure it's all a terrible mix up and there's no truth in it whatsoever.

JOE: None whatsoever.

Exit MRS CORDEN

Stall them, I'll hide the evidence.

KEN: Why, what can they do.

JOE: Punish us.

KEN: A minor misdemeanour, a schoolboy prank.

JOE: I take my writing seriously, very seriously indeed.

KEN: Nothing, they can do nothing, it's hardly a criminal matter.

JOE: A fine at the least.

KEN: A library fine. Who ever heard of anyone going to jail for scribbling in a library book.

JOE: They're not scribbles.

KEN: They'd have to lock up half the children in England.

JOE: They do lock up half the children in England.

KEN: How do I look.

JOE: Guilty.

KEN: *Vene, vidi, vicci.*

JOE: Like a lamb to the slaughter.

KEN: *O diem praeclarum.*

> *Exit KEN*

> *JOE clears the stage of evidence and exits*

TWO

> *Centre stage a battered brown suitcase*

> *Enter JOE with case*

JOE: Hello. Hello. Anyone at home?

> *JOE puts case on bed*

> *Toilet flushes*

> *Enter KEN*

KEN: John.

JOE: Ken.

> *Silence*

I got the train back to Victoria, and then the bus.

KEN: I waited for you at the bus station.

JOE: How was Brighton?

KEN: Oh, yes, a right regular bundle of laughs – Donkey rides on the beach, Max Miller at the Pavilion, fish and chips, the Aquarium, amusement arcades, swimming in the sea, ice-creams, candy floss and then back to the prison for tea. How was Brighton. How the bloody hell should I know,

I've been locked up all day, every day for the last six months – how about you.

JOE: All right, Kenneth I only asked.

KEN: I suppose HM Prison Eastchurch Kent was a bleeding holiday camp.

JOE: No.

Silence

I had to see the prison psychiatrist before I left.

KEN: What did he want.

JOE: He thought it his duty to warn me that you might be a homosexual.

KEN: What do they know. Bloody witch doctors.

JOE: You are a homosexual.

KEN: It's none of his business. I need a glass of water.

Exit KEN

JOE opens case takes out pile of papers and puts them next to typewriter

JOE: Six months, for six months I had a room of my own.

Enter KEN with glass of water and asprin

KEN: Six months, one day four hours and thirty-six minutes to be exact.

JOE: And privacy. They kept me in my cell for twenty-three hours a day. How about you?

KEN takes asprin and drinks water

I took it one day at a time.

KEN: So now you're the bird man of Alcatraz.

JOE: It wasn't so bad.

KEN: It was hell.

JOE: You had a room of your own.

KEN: We were locked up.

JOE: Three square meals a day. And wall to wall men.

KEN: You want me to be grateful.

JOE: It could have been worse.

KEN: I'm never going out again.

> *Knock at door*

VOICE: (*Off.*) It's only me.

KEN: That's all we need, as we cling to the raft of medusa – a visit from one of the furies.

VOICE: (*Off.*) Can I come in?

JOE: Come in, Mrs Corden.

> *Enter MRS CORDEN with bed linen*

MRS CORDEN: So, you're back.

KEN: Yes, we're back.

JOE: One of the best holidays I had.

MRS CORDEN: A new leaf.

JOE: Thanks for keeping an eye on the place for us.

MRS CORDEN: It's the least I could do. There's tea, milk, bread, sugar, margarine and a pound of cheese in the kitchen

JOE: Thank you.

> *MRS CORDEN puts sheets on the end of KEN's bed*

MRS CORDEN: You've lost weight Kenneth.

> *Puts sheets on JOE's bed*

KEN: We were persecuted.

MRS CORDEN: What for.

KEN: No crime, no crime whatsoever.

MRS CORDEN: Six months does seem an awfully long time for writing in a library book.

JOE: It wasn't just one, the prosecution cited nearly two hundred.

MRS CORDEN: Two hundred, they probably had to take on extra staff to deal with demand. You were providing employment.

KEN: My nerves are shot to pieces.

MRS CORDEN: You should see the doctor.

KEN: I'm not well enough.

MRS CORDEN: He'll give you something for them.

KEN: I don't want anything.

MRS CORDEN: Tablets. You can get tablets for everything nowadays. Mister Corden got some for his in-growing toenail.

KEN: I don't want tablets.

JOE: The judge, quite sensibly in my opinion, opted for a custodial sentence as a fine would have ruined us financially.

KEN: We are ruined financially.

JOE: Only because Islington Council is pursing us for damages.

KEN: Their pound of flesh.

MRS CORDEN: It's wicked. I hope the chief librarian's got children, that some terrible disaster befalls them, that they get taken away by the police, then he'll know misery and what it is to suffer. It'll be no good him crying to me over sour milk, the milk's already been spilt.

JOE: We appreciate your support, Mrs Corden.

MRS CORDEN: They could get rid of the public library, scrap the lot of them and I wouldn't care.

JOE: We emerge from the darkness.

KEN: Cursing God and man.

Silence

MRS CORDEN: Well, you're back now.

JOE: Yes, we're back.

MRS CORDEN: You've paid your debt to society.

KEN: We never owed it anything.

MRS CORDEN: You're secret's safe with me

KEN: It's not a secret, we're just not telling anyone.

MRS CORDEN: Well, there's clean sheets on your beds – the future might not be rosy but at least it's bright. Mr Corden and I want you to think of us like family.

JOE: We do Mrs Corden, we do.

MRS CORDEN: Well if you need anything.

JOE: Yes, thank you.

MRS CORDEN: Anything at all, you know where I am.

JOE: Yes.

MRS CORDEN: Don't hesitate.

JOE: No we won't.

MRS CORDEN: Well, I'll leave you in peace. I expect you've got a lot of catching up to do.

KEN: Yes, yes we have.

MRS CORDEN: We're glad to have you back.

JOE: Back on the straight and narrow.

MRS CORDEN: That's right, stick to the straight and narrow and you'll not go far wrong.

Exit MRS CORDEN

JOE: Yes, we will.

Closes door behind her as she goes

I will.

JOE crosses to desk and sits at typewriter
Threads a piece of paper off the desk and types

KEN: I'll put the kettle on.

JOE: Yes.

KEN: I will, I'll put the kettle on.

JOE: Yes, you do that.

JOE types

KEN: I'll go and put the kettle on.

Exit KEN

JOE finishes the line he is typing and then reads back what he's written

JOE: (*Reads.*) 'Scene one. A bed/living room, with a sink in it. Mike is shaving at the sink.'

Stops reading
Looks up around the room as if for inspiration
Then speaks as he types

Joyce enters carrying a tray –

Re-enter KEN

JOE continues typing

KEN: I've put the kettle on.

> *JOE keeps typing*

What are you doing.

JOE: Something I started in prison.

KEN: Work.

JOE: Yes.

KEN: Ah, work, where do we begin – shall I extemporise
– places – but first I must know what we're writing about.

JOE: We're not, I am.

KEN: You don't want me to work.

JOE: You write what you like, I'm doing this on my own.

> *JOE types*

KEN: You've never written anything before without telling me
first.

JOE: Kenneth.

KEN: All right.

> *JOE types*

You could at least tell me the title.

> *JOE stops typing*

JOE: *Ruffian on the Stair*, satisfied?

KEN: That's one of our titles.

JOE: Yes, and now I'm using it.

KEN: All right, all right. I'm sorry I spoke.

JOE: You soon will be.

KEN: Why, what are you going to do.

JOE: I'll hit you.

KEN: You wouldn't.

JOE: No

KEN: No.

JOE: Try me.

KEN: You wouldn't.

JOE: I bloody well will if you don't stop.

KEN: I'm not doing anything.

JOE: I'm trying to work.

KEN: What's stopping you.

JOE: You are.

KEN: No, I'm not.

JOE: Yes you are.

KEN: No I'm not.

JOE: You bloody well are Kenneth.

KEN: So, what are you going to do about it?

JOE: Nothing.

> *JOE types*

KEN: You couldn't.

JOE: Any time I want.

> *JOE types*

KEN: Golden bollocks.

JOE: Right.

> *JOE chases KEN*
> *Pins him to floor and tickles him*

KEN: No, no – don't – stop – I can't breath – no – don't –
please, stop, stop it, please.

JOE: Give in. Give in. Give in.

KEN: Never.

> *JOE rolls off*

I didn't give in.

JOE: I know.

KEN: Sadist.

JOE: Masochist.

> *JOE sits back at desk*

KEN: You're no fun.

JOE: You're no fun.

> *JOE types*

KEN: You've changed.

> *JOE stops typing*

JOE: And you haven't. The old whore society lifted up her
skirts to us and the stench was revolting. There's nothing
more she can do to us, we're untouchable.

> *JOE turns to resume typing*
> *Stops*
> *Stands*

KEN: Finished.

JOE: No.

> *JOE paces*
> *Stares at paper in typewriter*
> *Pulls it out screws it up and throws it away*

Rubbish.

JOE inserts another sheet
Types

KEN: What about me.

JOE: Read a book.

KEN: I don't want to read a book.

JOE: Go out.

KEN: I'm never going out again.

JOE: Then stay in.

KEN: I'll make the tea.

JOE: Stop complaining.

KEN: I'm not. I don't.

JOE: You do. It's what you do best.

KEN: You've got no heart.

JOE: That's right, it's pure muscle

JOE continues typing

KEN: It's not good. I'm not good. It's not right, this is not right,
I don't feel right.

JOE: See a doctor then.

KEN: I do, I feel bad, really bad. I'll go to the doctor. I will.
I am. Get him to give me something for my nerves.

JOE: Yes, you do that.

KEN: Some tablets, that's what I need.

JOE: Yes, tablets.

KEN: I am, I'm going. I'll go. What are you doing.

JOE: Working. And then I might take a stroll up to the pissoir
on the corner of Islington Green.

KEN: You always go to such interesting places.

> *Exit KEN*

JOE: Yes, yes.

> *Stops typing and reads*

Got it. 'Have you got an appointment today?', 'Yes. I'm to be at King's Cross station at eleven. I'm meeting a man in the toilet.' Got you.

> *JOE types and speaks the line*

'You always go to such interesting places.' Thank you, Kenneth.

> *JOE puts on jacket*
> *Smothers face in baby lotion*
> *Checks himself in mirror*
> *And exits*
>
> *As the lights fade and change for the next scene we hear music from* Pal Joey *playing*

THREE

> *Light up on the set*
> *Door leading to kitchen open*
> Pal Joey *playing on the record player*
>
> *Loud crash of breaking crockery from kitchen*

KEN: (*Offstage.*) Damn sink.

> *Enter KEN in a pinny wearing rubber gloves holding a plunger*

Bloody music.

> *Turns off record player*
>
> *Knock at the door*

(*Shouts at door.*) Now what.

VOICE: (*Off.*) It's only me.

KEN: Oh, Mrs Corden, hang on.

> *He throws plunger on bed and starts to take off gloves*
>
> *Knocking*

I'm coming.

VOICE: (*Off.*) It's me Mrs Corden.

KEN: (*Taking off gloves.*) Yes, I know.

MRS CORDEN: (*Off.*) It's urgent.

KEN: I'm not decent.

> *Throws gloves on his bed*

MRS CORDEN: (*Off.*) Well how decent are you?

KEN: Half decent –

> *Undoing pinny*

MRS CORDEN: (*Off.*) That'll do.

> *Enter MRS CORDEN with a letter*
>
> *As she enters KEN pulls off pinny and throws it on bed*

It's a letter.

KEN: There, I'm decent now.

MRS CORDEN: A letter from the BBC. It's for John.

KEN: He's out.

MRS CORDEN: I know. I'll wait. It's not every day that a letter from the British Broadcasting Corporation arrives through your letter box.

KEN: Just leave it on his bed.

MRS CORDEN: It might be important.

KEN: I'll make sure he gets it.

MRS CORDEN: I don't mind waiting. I've been on the edge of my seat ever since it arrived.

She sits

They've got his name wrong. It's addressed to Joe Orton, not John.

KEN: A clerical error.

MRS CORDEN: You think.

KEN: I do.

MRS CORDEN: That's not the sort of thing you expect from the BBC is it?

KEN: I expect nothing.

MRS CORDEN: I heard John go out this morning. It came in the second post. I couldn't wait any longer.

KEN: He won't be long now.

MRS CORDEN: There's a pair of rubber gloves and a plunger on your bed.

KEN: Yes. I'm washing up.

MRS CORDEN: In bed. I've interrupted you.

KEN: No, no.

MRS CORDEN: Say no more Kenneth, I am a woman of the modern world.

Silence

It might be to do with his play, he's sold a play to the radio.

KEN: Yes, I know, we keep no secrets.

MRS CORDEN: It's called *The Ruffian on the Stair*. What an imagination.

KEN: *Ruffian on the Stair*. One of my titles.

MRS CORDEN: Imagine that, a play on the radio.

KEN: Yes. We work very much together.

MRS CORDEN: Oh, yes I know, you're very close.

Enter JOE

KEN: Mrs Corden's got a letter for you.

MRS CORDEN: From the BBC. It came in the second post. I hope you don't mind but I wanted to deliver it in person.

JOE: Thank you.

MRS CORDEN: There's been a clerical error, they've got your name wrong. Most unlike the BBC.

JOE: No, that's right, Joe Orton. I've changed my name.

MRS CORDEN: Over night.

KEN: Just like that, without consulting me.

JOE: Yes. Joe Orton – why not, I've re-invented myself, so why not the name as well.

MRS CORDEN: I like the name Joe, it's a good honest name – Joseph was a carpenter.

KEN: Cuckolded by God, and then the baby came along, he said, 'That's rather odd'.

MRS CORDEN: I do, I like it, it's honest.

KEN: Like Stalin, good old honest uncle Joe. You get a play on the radio and you change your name.

JOE: Yes.

MRS CORDEN: It's not everyone can get a play on the radio Kenneth.

KEN: No, no it's not.

Silence

36

Well, I'll get back in the kitchen where I'm needed the most.

> *KEN picks up rubber gloves, plunger and pinny*
> *Exit KEN into kitchen*

MRS CORDEN: You're not opening your letter.

JOE: No.

MRS CORDEN: Savouring it for later.

JOE: Yes. (*JOE lowers voice.*) Mrs Corden I need your help.

MRS CORDEN: Well, if I can.

JOE: You see I'm expecting a visitor.

MRS CORDEN: For tea.

JOE: No. A lady.

MRS CORDEN: Oh, that is unusual.

JOE: Yes.

MRS CORDEN: Mr Corden and I, we never had you down as the marrying type.

JOE: No, it's business.

MRS CORDEN: Not bad news I hope.

JOE: No, no – I've got an agent.

MRS CORDEN: You're not in trouble again.

JOE: No, not that sort of an agent, a literary agent. She's going to represent me. It was her that got me to change my name.

MRS CORDEN: How thrilling.

JOE: Yes, and she's coming to take me to dinner but I haven't told Kenneth yet.

MRS CORDEN: He'll be delighted.

JOE: Over the moon.

MRS CORDEN: You think he might take against her.

> *KEN appears in doorway to kitchen and holds up a tin in either hand*

KEN: Pilchards in tomato sauce or tinned salmon.

JOE: Pilchards.

KEN: Your wish is my command.

> *Exit KEN*

MRS CORDEN: Tinned salmon, you are coming up in the world.

JOE: So when she arrives.

MRS CORDEN: Your agent.

JOE: I want you to tell her to wait downstairs, and then come and get me. She'll be here about six thirty.

MRS CORDEN: Six thirty.

JOE: Yes, six thirty. But don't tell Kenneth.

MRS CORDEN: Don't tell Kenneth.

JOE: Just come and fetch me.

MRS CORDEN: Come and fetch you.

JOE: I want it to be a suprise.

MRS CORDEN: An agent.

JOE: Yes.

MRS CORDEN: A secret agent.

JOE: That's right.

MRS CORDEN: Like in the films. Imagine, coming to our front door. I've never met an agent before, but how would you know, if they're secret – I could have met dozens unwittingly – what do they do.

JOE: Contracts.

MRS CORDEN: It's probably best I don't know any more.

JOE: You won't say a word.

MRS CORDEN: My lips are sealed. Oh, John, you and Kenneth do lead such interesting lives.

Exit MRS CORDEN

JOE sits at desk and types

Enter KEN with newspaper

KEN: You're not going to open your letter.

JOE: Later.

KEN sits on bed

KEN: (*Reads from newspaper.*) 'Man dies of electric shock while attempting sex with standard lamp'.

JOE: Stupid twat.

KEN: He wired up his testicles to a standard lamp and then plugged it in.

JOE: Just read your paper.

KEN: I am.

JOE types

But what prompted you to change your name.

JOE: Read your paper.

KEN: I am.

JOE types

KEN reads

Silence

Maybe finally the time has come for me to admit I've got nothing to say.

JOE: Or maybe you've just decided finally to say nothing.

KEN: 'The crest over over-reached, then the going down again.'

JOE: Samuel Beckett.

KEN: Matthew Arnold.

> *KEN picks up letter*
> *JOE snatches it back and continues to work*

I'm worn out with waiting.

JOE: 'For better or worse there's nothing in life that doesn't come to an end sooner or later.'

KEN: Charles Dickens, *Bleak House*. You have to get up earlier than that if you want to catch me. Just because you've sold a play.

JOE: It's only the radio.

KEN: No, I'm happy for you.

JOE: I'm not asking you to be.

KEN: Well I am. It's only by the success of others that we can truly be sure of our own failure.

JOE: Kenneth.

KEN: What are you doing.

JOE: Writing.

KEN: Of course. The writer must write.

> *JOE works*

'The distances I travel each night, that lonely sojourn between sunrise and the gloom of midnight, where hope becomes a twilight memory sinking before the oncoming of the utter dark.'

JOE: James Joyce.

KEN: Kenneth Halliwell.

JOE: Oh, I give up.

KEN: No, don't let me stop you from working. Open your letter.

JOE works

There is an argument to say that the British theatre has gone downhill ever since the introduction of women.

JOE: Shakespeare didn't know he was born.

KEN: I do hope I've written nothing as bad as Shakespeare's early plays. It's all over. And now? The British stage is awash with Kitchen Sink drama – crawling with Oxbridge graduates like flies round a cows arse, second rate talentless mediocrities who've never had an original idea in their lives – queer bent bastards who wouldn't know a masterpiece if it fell into their pre-priapic laps – all washing down the inequities of the class system in the circle bar with a glass of cool white or jolly red and a pretty young blonde.

JOE: What have you got against blondes?

KEN: Nothing. God is a gentleman and he prefers blondes.

JOE: I wish somebody would write a play about our kitchen sink.

KEN: The only thing they'd find of any interest would be your underpants.

JOE: They could tell a story or two.

JOE works

KEN: And I can't stand the Opera.

JOE: You don't like anything.

KEN: As that enlightened master of wit and social satire says, 'Anything too silly to be said can always be sung'.

JOE: Noël Coward.

KEN: Voltaire. You look anxious, as though you've got some bad news to impart.

JOE: No.

KEN: Good, it wouldn't do for a successful author with an about-to-be-produced radio play to be anxious.

JOE: I'm trying to work.

KEN: Pardon me if I breathed. You've got nothing to tell.

JOE: No.

KEN: You're sure.

JOE: What, what I have got to tell.

KEN: I don't know, you haven't told me, yet.

JOE: There's nothing to tell, all right.

KEN: All right. You look guilty.

JOE: Kenneth.

KEN: Your ears have gone red.

JOE: It's hot, I'm hot.

KEN: We'll go for a walk.

JOE: No.

KEN: Why don't you want to open your letter. Open your letter. Are you sure you don't want to go for a walk?

JOE: Absolutely.

KEN: What's in your letter?

JOE: I give up.

KEN: Don't let me stop you from working.

JOE: It's like living with a woman.

KEN: What's wrong with women?

JOE: Nothing, but one of the principal reasons I'm homosexual is that I like men. I'm not interested in any man that behaves like a woman.

KEN: You're the one that smothers his face in baby lotion not me.

JOE: I like to be lubricated when I go out the house. Prepared for any chance encounter.

KEN: What about me?

JOE: You don't like sex.

KEN: I like sex.

JOE: You require at least a week's notice in order to get an erection, by which time all the fun's gone out of it.

KEN: It's these tablets they've given me.

JOE: No, it's you.

KEN: For my nerves.

JOE: It's you. And because you can't –

KEN: You take me for granted.

JOE: Because you won't, you think I shouldn't.

KEN: There's more to life than just sex.

JOE: What do you want us to do, settle down and have children.

> *Knock at door*

MRS CORDEN: (*Off.*) It's only me.

43

Enter MRS CORDEN

Those stairs they'll be the death of me. I'm sorry to interrupt boys, only it's six thirty, mister Corden's still not back from work and I'm in the middle of making him a steak and kidney pudding and I can't go out – it's six thirty, and I was wondering if one of you boys could run an errand for me.

KEN: I'll go, what is it you want.

JOE: No, no, it's all right, I'll go.

MRS CORDEN: Yes, John, you go – I wouldn't want you putting yourself to any trouble on my account, Kenneth.

KEN: It's no trouble, I could do with the walk.

JOE: You've had all day to go for a walk.

KEN: You don't want me to go.

JOE: No, no, you go.

KEN: We'll go together.

MRS CORDEN: No.

JOE: No, I'll stay and work.

KEN: What do you want.

MRS CORDEN: Oh –... er... I forgot coming up the stairs – oh, yes, a packet of Bird's custard powder.

JOE: Is there anything downstairs waiting for me to pick it up, Mrs Corden?

MRS CORDEN: Oh, yes, there is – completely slipped my mind, what with mister Corden's steak and kidney pudding – a package, from a lady.

KEN: How do you know.

MRS CORDEN: She's delivered it in person, specifically asking for Joe Orton.

KEN: Joe.

MRS CORDEN: Yes, John. And she's waiting downstairs in my front room.

JOE: Tell her I'll be down, right away.

MRS CORDEN: I must say, she doesn't look very secretive, rather a plain looking woman if you ask me. No need for the custard powder, I remember I got a packet on Monday.

Exit MRS CORDEN

KEN: You know this woman.

JOE: Yes. She's taking me to dinner.

KEN: What about your pilchards.

JOE: She's an agent, I was meaning to tell you.

KEN: She wants to represent us.

JOE: No, me.

KEN: I'm pleased for you. Very pleased.

JOE: She's keen to read some of your stuff.

KEN: She knows who I am.

JOE: Yes, I told her you're my literary father figure.

KEN: You make me sound like a rather dull Ezra Pound to your dazzling Eliot.

JOE: Verlaine and Rimbaud.

KEN: Thanks, now I get to be the middle-aged soak to youthful genius.

JOE: I'll take my letter.

KEN: For her professional opinion.

JOE: Yes.

KEN: What's her name.

JOE: Peggy.

KEN: Peggy. Another parasite living off the back of the artist.

JOE: You don't know her.

KEN: I don't like her.

JOE: You've never met her.

KEN: So you're not going to eat in.

JOE: No.

KEN: You're not going to invite your new friend up.

JOE: She's not a friend, she's my agent.

KEN: So you keep saying.

JOE: The way you're going on anybody would think I had a mistress.

KEN: Where are you going?

JOE: I don't know. Out with my agent.

KEN: Peggy.

JOE: Yes.

KEN: I'll save you some pilchards.

JOE: Don't, don't do this to me Ken.

KEN: I'm not doing anything.

JOE: Don't come the mater bloody dolorosa with me.

> *Exit JOE*

> *KEN takes a tablet*

> *Between the end of this scene and the next the beginning of the collage, suddenly an explosion of images on the wall.*

FOUR (1)

KEN standing on his bed, a stack of magazines by his bedside,
pasting cut-out images onto the wall
Listening to 'What is a Man', Pal Joey

Enter JOE with box

JOE: Don't you ever get tired of listening to this.

KEN: No. It's like a friend, the only difference is I always know
    where to find it and it never lets me down.

JOE: You need to get out.

KEN: I like it in.

JOE: Well, I'm here now.

> *Turns off music*

We had John Gieulgud and Harold Pinter watching today
and there's talk of taking the play to Broadway.

KEN: Cricklewood or Ealing. Did you get any milk.

JOE: Of course I told them the Americans won't like it.

KEN: We need milk.

JOE: *Entertaining Mister Sloane* on Broadway –

KEN: How entertaining.

JOE: Not bad for a boy from the Saffron Lane Estate.

KEN: You didn't get any milk.

JOE: We're going to New York.

KEN: Are we.

JOE: You haven't been out today.

KEN: I'm pleased for you, very pleased, I'm sure you'll be a
    big success on Broadway.

JOE: I went to the bank today and withdrew against my first royalty cheque for *Entertaining Mister Sloane*.

KEN puts cut out image against the wall

KEN: What do you think.

JOE: You're obsessed with that wall.

KEN: It can be relied on.

JOE: You need to get out.

KEN: What's in the box.

JOE: A present.

KEN: For your agent, to thank your agent.

JOE: No. It's for you.

KEN: More good news.

JOE: Go on, open it.

KEN: What is it?

JOE: Open it, open it and see.

KEN opens box and takes out a wig

Put it on.

It's a wig.

KEN: Yes, I know. I know what a wig looks like.

JOE: It's a present, I bought it for you. Put it on.

I got it from Stanlee's – with two e's – of Paris on the Essex Road, just up past the taxidermist. Put it on.

KEN puts on wig

Well.

KEN: No. I can't.

JOE: You haven't seen yourself.

KEN: A boiled egg with a tea cosy on its crown.

JOE: Put it back on and look at me.

KEN: No, I can't.

JOE: Do it.

> *KEN puts wig on*
>
> *JOE straightens it for him*

There.

KEN: It's no good.

JOE: Why not.

KEN: I feel like a depressed monkey with a rug on its head.

JOE: You're not trying.

KEN: I'm trying.

JOE: Put it on again. And this time with conviction.

> *KEN puts wig on*

Stop frowning.

KEN: I'm not.

JOE: You are. Smile. That's better. Now look at me in the eyes and tell me what you want.

KEN: I don't know, what do I want.

JOE: Sex.

KEN: Oh, yes.

JOE: So, tell me.

KEN: I want sex.

JOE: No, not like that. Seduce me.

KEN: How about it then. A spot of the other.

JOE: No, not like that. Tell me you need me.

KEN: I need you.

JOE: No, say it, really say it.

KEN: I need you,

JOE: And again like you mean it.

KEN: I do.

JOE: Then say it.

KEN: I need you.

JOE: Now tell me what you want.

KEN: You.

JOE: No, tell me what you want.

KEN: I do, I want you. What do you want.

JOE: Yeah, it works, it really does work with a wig on.

KEN: What do you want John, you haven't said, you've got to say.

JOE: Come on, let's go out and give it a try in public – see if we can't find you a nice bit of trade.

KEN: Your attitude to life, sex and art is the same as Dr Arnold's – just get out there on the Victorian playing fields of England and do it. If only it were that easy.

JOE: Have as much fun with your genitalia as you can while you're still alive or you'll regret it after.
With that wig on the world's your oyster.

KEN: I don't like oysters.

JOE sits on bed

JOE: You don't want the wig.

KEN: You, you…you –

JOE: What about me.

KEN: You're so, so infantile, infuriating, in love with yourself.

JOE: I'll take the wig back, then.

KEN: I didn't say that.

JOE: Good. Let's take it out and give it a trial run in the pissoir on the corner of Islington Green.

KEN: No.

JOE: Come on, you know you want to.

KEN: No, I don't.

JOE: Spoilsport.

KEN: You go out.

JOE: Yes, I will, now I've given my legs a rest.

KEN: Animal.

JOE: It's you in your wig it's got me going.

KEN: I see your game.

JOE: There is no game, I've got this overwhelming urge to have sex with a stranger.

KEN: You're sick you know that.

JOE: Yes, I can sexualise anything, even a door knob.

KEN: I have no wish to know.

JOE: Success, it's an aphrodisiac. You're staying in.

KEN: Yes, I am.

JOE: All right, keep your wig on.

KEN: That sort of comment is the reason why your plays are so cheap.

JOE: I'm going then.

KEN: You go, see if I care.

> *KEN sits at typewriter*

I've started work on the new play.

JOE: What new play?

KEN: Our new play.

JOE: My new play.

KEN: The new play we discussed.

JOE: No, Kenneth, it's my play – we talked about it, I talked to you about my idea for a new play, that doesn't make it yours. If you want to write a play write one of your own. *Funeral Games* is my play.

KEN: *Loot*'s a much better title.

JOE: So you say.

KEN: I do, it has more of a 'thirties whodunit feel about it that fits with the genre we're writing in.

JOE: But it's still my play.

KEN: And I've worked out where the crooks should stash their loot – in the dead mother's coffin.

JOE: That's brilliant.

KEN: You don't admit it, you never admit to it in public, the help I give you – you couldn't write the plays you do but for me.

JOE: I dedicated *Sloane* to you, what more do you want? I'm going.

KEN: Where are you going.

JOE: Out. I'm going out.

> *Exit JOE*

KEN: No, John, wait –… John.

Between this scene and the next more images appear on the wall. As they do the lights change from day to night, indicating a passage of time taking us into the next scene.

FOUR (2)

MRS CORDEN and KEN cleaning up the room

MRS CORDEN: I see you've had a telephone installed.

KEN: Yes, John felt we needed one.

MRS CORDEN: It's no good trying to ring us we don't have a phone.

KEN: It was for work. But the tour of *Loot* has been such a disaster that I shouldn't wonder we'll get rid of it.

MRS CORDEN: Poor lamb, the reviews have been bad.

KEN: Atrocious. I can hardly bring myself to repeat them.

MRS CORDEN: Nobody believes what they read in the papers anyway.

KEN: Some of them are so vicious I can't get them out of my head, 'An evening of very British rubbish', the *Cambridge Post.*

MRS CORDEN: Oh, that's not fair.

KEN: No and it gets worse, 'Damp Squib for West End sponge', the *Oxford Bugle.*

MRS CORDEN: Poor thing.

KEN: 'Bournemouth old ladies shocked', *The Times.*

MRS CORDEN: Serves them right for going.

KEN: Wimbledon's the worst, 'The most revolting play I've ever seen'.

MRS CORDEN: Oh, how I wish I'd got to see it.

SIMON BENT

KEN: It's a great big flop.

MRS CORDEN: Fame is such a fleeting thing.

KEN: We always knew it wouldn't last, I tried to prepare John for this but he was so gung-ho.

MRS CORDEN: You think it won't go into the West End.

KEN: Not with notices like those. I'm afraid we've had our success.

MRS CORDEN: That's a shame, Mr Corden promised me a new frock.

KEN: We all have our disappointments to bear.

MRS CORDEN: Still he's done well.

KEN: More than any of us could have reasonably expected. Wimbledon was the last nail in the coffin.

MRS CORDEN: Did he pass his eleven plus?

KEN: No, I don't think so.

MRS CORDEN: Oh, he has done well for himself then.

KEN: He's punch-drunk with all the re-writes, the producer's have had him up working night and day.

MRS CORDEN: A play on the radio, a play in the West End and he probably studied wood-work.

KEN: He's typed his fingers to the bone.

MRS CORDEN: What for?

KEN: A last minute bid to save himself.

MRS CORDEN: Failure, it's a bitter pill to swallow Kenneth.

KEN: He'll be inconsolable.

MRS CORDEN: You don't know what it's like.

KEN: Oh, yes I do Mrs Corden. Rejection, it's the lot of every true artist.

Takes out a letter from a draw

I keep this letter as a constant reminder.

MRS CORDEN: Who's it from.

KEN: Peggy Ramsay.

MRS CORDEN: John's Agent.

KEN: This what she has to say about my play *The Facts of Life,* (*Reads.*) 'Kenneth, I haven't really got through your adaptation. The first scene sent me into such a well of boredom that I had to struggle to continue which I did in a kind of abstract anguish.'

MRS CORDEN: Who's she to say anything.

KEN: London's most powerful play agent, a failed opera singer, a woman whose theatrical career started with clowning in pantomime, a woman of whom it can be truly said she started at the bottom.

MRS CORDEN: You're not appreciated Kenneth, you need appreciating.

KEN: Van Gogh never sold a painting in his life.

MRS CORDEN: And now they give him away with tubes of toothpaste, if you collect the coupons. There's no future in it, you should get out now Kenneth while you still can – become a teacher.

KEN: I'm afraid it's too late Mrs Corden, mine and John's lot is cast, to struggle on to the bitter end.

MRS CORDEN: Oh, well, at least you'll have a bit of company in your old age.

KEN: Yes.

MRS CORDEN: No, it's no good trying to ring us we don't have a phone.

KEN: He'll be desolate.

MRS CORDEN: You've got family you can ring Kenneth.

KEN: A few long distance relatives, nothing much.

I'm very short on family.

MRS CORDEN: What time are you expecting him?

KEN: Soon.

MRS CORDEN: You should put your wig on.

KEN: I save it for special occasions.

MRS CORDEN: This is a special occasion.

KEN: Birthdays, Christmas, holidays, that sort of thing.

MRS CORDEN: I hope you don't mind me asking, but what age did it start to drop out?

KEN: It didn't.

MRS CORDEN: You keep it like that by choice.

KEN: Yes I shave my head.

MRS CORDEN: You shave your head?

KEN: Yes I prefer it that way. It's cooler.

MRS CORDEN: So you don't need a wig?

KEN: It's a luxury

MRS CORDEN: Mr Corden and I were only remarking the other day how handsome you look in it, a real matinee idol film star looks.

Enter JOE with case

Oh, hello John.

JOE: Hello, Mrs Corden.

> *Crosses to bed and sits on it*

I'm beat.

> *Lies on bed*

I just want to curl up and die.

> *Curls up on bed*

MRS CORDEN: I'll leave you two to it.

KEN: (*Whispers.*) Yes, yes, I'll see to him now.

> *Exit MRS CORDEN*
>
> *KEN sits on end of bed*

JOE: It's all over.

KEN: It's all right, you're home now.

JOE: I've got nothing left.

KEN: You've got me.

> *Silence*

You and me.

> *Silence*

We've got each other.

> *Silence*

Together. Sod them, sod them all if they can't take a joke.

JOE: Don't let the bastards grind you down.

KEN: That's the spirit, John and Kenneth *contra mundem.* What they don't know is that you can just stop. You don't give a damn. We know what rejection is. We've faced it before and we'll face it again – together.

JOE: Us and them.

KEN: That's right.

JOE: The next play I write, I wont send it to anyone, I'll just keep it stashed at the bottom of my drawer.

KEN: Why bother to write it at all.

JOE: To hell with them.

KEN: That's right. You know I've always admired the way Rimbaud and Congreve just stopped writing. We could inform the papers.

JOE: I don't know, I don't know.

KEN: What would Mrs Dale say, go on.

JOE: 'Selly, I'm awfully worried about Jim –'

KEN: 'I can't find him anywhere, he's gone missing along with the broom handle and the jar of Vaseline from under our bed. I do hope he's not up to his old tricks again.'

> *Phone rings*

Ignore it. Best to ignore it. It'll only be some nobody wanting to speak to Joe Orton

JOE: It might be Peggy.

KEN: Leave it.

> *Both look at phone*
> *It continues to ring*
> *The phone stops ringing*

See nothing, now you sleep.

JOE: Yes, I'll sleep.

KEN: Sleep.

> *JOE turns over*

> *KEN runs his hand along JOE's back just hovering above it*

I'll be in the kitchen.

KEN turns off light

The light from the kitchen shines through the doorway

KEN goes over to phone
Picks up receiver
And leaves it off the hook
Then crosses to doorway

We're back together again. You and me.

Exit KEN
Closing the door behind him

Darkness

Interval

Act Two

Phone ringing

Enter KEN from kitchen
Dressed half smart
Carrying a plate of sliced battenburg and a pot of tea
Doesn't know where to put them

KEN: Bugger.

Puts plate on JOE's bed
And pot on desk
Picks up phone

Hello. Hello.

Puts phone down

Bugger. (*Shouts off.*) John. I've made a pot of tea. You can't stay in there all day, you'll be late. Your public needs you. (*Aside.*) Like a hole in the head.

Slips record out of its sleeve

My old pal Joey.

Puts record on
'That Terrific Rainbow', Pal Joey

KEN looks at himself in the mirror
Unimpressed he crosses to his bed and takes a tablet
Puts on his wig
Crosses to look at himself in mirror
Stops midway
Turns back and takes another tablet
Goes back to mirror
Turns sideways
Pulls his stomach in
Then lets it out deflated

Straightens JOE's bed

As he does toilet flushes

Enter JOE in shirt underpants shoes and socks

JOE: What are you doing?

KEN: Pouring the tea.

JOE turns off record player

JOE: Who was that on the telephone?

KEN: Nobody.

JOE: It might have been Peggy.

KEN: It wasn't anybody.

JOE: It must have been somebody. It might have been important.

KEN: They'll ring back.

JOE: There's a plate of Battenburg on my bed.

KEN: I bought it to celebrate. It's not every day you get to go to Quaglinos and pick up an Evening Standard award for best play.

JOE picks up plate

JOE: Is this a form of attack.

KEN: No it's Battenburg. As Freud said, sometimes a cigar is just a cigar.

JOE: You're doing this to punish me. You said you didn't want to go.

KEN: Wild horses wouldn't drag me to such a macabre event.

JOE: Where's your suit?

KEN: With Mrs Corden.

JOE: What's Mrs Corden got it for?

KEN: She's attacking some rather virulent gravy stains.

JOE: Where is she, where is it, I'm going to be late.

KEN: If you're going to get in such a state I'll have to come with you.

JOE: No, you won't, I'm taking Peggy and that's final.

MRS CORDEN: (*Off.*) It's only me.

KEN: I never wanted to go in the first place.

Enter MRS CORDEN with suit

MRS CORDEN: Oh, John. I don't know where to look. I like your shoes.

JOE: Thank you, Mrs Corden. I'll take the suit.

MRS CORDEN: Hush puppies.

JOE: Yes.

Takes suit

Thank you.

MRS CORDEN: Are they comfortable.

KEN: Yes, quite.

MRS CORDEN: I believe they're all the rage, with the young men of today.

KEN: Have some Battenburg.

MRS CORDEN: No, no thank you.

JOE: She's watching her figure.

MRS CORDEN: I'm glad to see you're wearing clean underwear for the occasion, John.

KEN: You could practise your speech on Mrs Corden.

MRS CORDEN: I always make sure Mr Corden's wearing clean underwear, in case of an emergency, I wouldn't want him disgracing himself.

KEN: What emergency?

MRS CORDEN: This is a public event, anything could happen.

KEN: It's only the Evening Standard awards.

JOE: You're just jealous.

KEN: Jealous, what's to be jealous of?

MRS CORDEN: And if they do have to rush you to hospital –

JOE: That I'm taking Peggy and not you.

MRS CORDEN: Don't let them rush you to the Whittington.

KEN: I'm not jealous of Peggy – I like Peggy she's very supportive – not just you, both of us – Peggy likes me, she just doesn't like my writing.

MRS CORDEN: Go to the Whittington and you're dead.

JOE: You are, you're jealous.

KEN: I'm not jealous.

MRS CORDEN: The woman on the corner went in on Wednesday complaining of a headache and was dead by Saturday. That hospital, it's rife with death.

JOE: You said you didn't want to come.

KEN: I don't. I just don't see why you have to go.

MRS CORDEN: Don't be silly Kenneth he's won an award for his play. Who'd have thought after it did so badly in Bournemouth and Oxford.

JOE: That was the tour of *Loot.*

MRS CORDEN: And Wimbledon found it revolting.

JOE: This is the London production of *Loot.*

MRS CORDEN: You had a star in it and it was a flop, and now there's no one in it that anyone's ever heard of it's a hit.

JOE: You can't come, I'm wearing your suit.

KEN: It doesn't fit me anyway.

JOE: It must have shrunk in the wash.

MRS CORDEN: Who'd have thought, a play about a son and his dead mother would win an award.

KEN: It's a Freudian nightmare.

JOE: Well what do you think

JOE now dressed

MRS CORDEN: You'll never get a girlfriend wearing shoes like that.

KEN: We don't want any.

MRS CORDEN: No, you've got your work.

JOE: When I was a boy we were lucky if we had shoes.

KEN: Oh, he tells such lies –

JOE: I don't tell lies, it's the truth.

KEN: You were not neglected as a child. You still go back to your mother's every summer.

JOE: Not this summer I won't, my mother's dead. I just need my father to die and I'll be an orphan like you.

MRS CORDEN: Your mother and father are dead, Kenneth.

JOE: Ken's an orphan.

MRS CORDEN: Oh, I am sorry.

KEN: Why, you didn't know them did you.

MRS CORDEN: God took your parents.

KEN: No, they died.

MRS CORDEN: Together, in the usual manner or was it an accident.

KEN: Yes and no.

MRS CORDEN: They were escaping some terrible threat.

KEN: No.

MRS CORDEN: The tragedy of it.

KEN: My mother was killed by a wasp, my father died a few years later.

MRS CORDEN: He couldn't go on.

KEN: No.

MRS CORDEN: The wait was too much for him.

KEN: Yes.

MRS CORDEN: I know how he felt.

JOE: Have some Battenburg.

MRS CORDEN: No.

JOE: Go on, it'll cheer you up.

MRS CORDEN: I couldn't.

KEN: I was seventeen, I came downstairs and found him dead with his head in the oven.

MRS CORDEN: Killed by the Gas Board.

JOE offers plate

JOE: Go on.

MRS CORDEN: No.

KEN: I turned off the gas, stepped over his body, made a cup of tea, went upstairs, shaved, washed, dressed then knocked on next door and asked to borrow their telephone. We didn't have one. To call the ambulance.

MRS CORDEN: Well at least you've got a telephone now.

JOE: Go on, have a piece. It's an exceptional bit of Battenburg, though I say it myself.

MRS CORDEN: Well just the one.

JOE: Only the best.

MRS CORDEN: I wouldn't want you to think I was unappreciative.

KEN: There was no rush.

Silence

MRS CORDEN: We've always had electricity.

JOE: Put temptation out of reach.

MRS CORDEN: It's cleaner.

JOE: I suppose giving a gas oven to someone with suicidal tendencies is like handing a psychopath a gun and saying you don't have to use it if you don't want.

MRS CORDEN: The Gas Board should only issue ovens to people of sound mental health.

JOE: Yes, but how would you know.

MRS CORDEN: It's tragic, very tragic. Life is tragedy.

Silence

Never have children Kenneth.

KEN: No, I won't.

MRS CORDEN: Never grow old.

KEN: My parents have set me a good example.

MRS CORDEN: The only hope left for a woman my age is the grave.

Silence

How's your writing going Ken.

KEN: Oh, it's…

JOE: Ken's moved into art full time, he does collages.

MRS CORDEN: Still, I expect he'll work his way up to Universities eventually, a man of your education Kenneth.

JOE: Collages, like the wall and the naked man on the bathroom ceiling.

MRS CORDEN: I'm very partial to him. Very modern. Have you got any drawings?

KEN: No. I've come to the startling conclusion that there is no such thing as a line in nature – a line is man's attempt to capture the effect of light on substance, therefore I have chosen to do away with drawing entirely and to juxtapose ready made images, creating from their collision new meaning.

MRS CORDEN: I suppose one writer in the room is enough.

JOE: Yes.

KEN: I shall make my way selling collages.

MRS CORDEN: Don't be silly Kenneth, you can't sell a wall.

KEN: No, I do smaller ones, with frames and behind glass. This is my masterpiece.

MRS CORDEN: Have you met with much success?

KEN: Some.

MRS CORDEN: How many have you sold?

KEN: None.

JOE: One actually, my agent bought one.

MRS CORDEN: That's very good of her.

KEN: Yes, it is, it's very good of her.

MRS CORDEN: I expect her support means a lot.

KEN: Inestimable. No, I mean that, I really mean it.

JOE: Speaking of which, she'll be waiting for me.

KEN: Let her wait.

JOE: I have to go.

KEN: I'll put a record on.

JOE: No, not now.

KEN: We're having a party.

> *KEN puts on record*
> *'Devil in Disguise', Elvis Presley*

JOE: I have to go.

MRS CORDEN: Think of the neighbours.

KEN: You are the neighbours.

> *KENNETH starts to dance*

Let go, the Lord of Misrule, gorge yourself, satiate the senses –

MRS CORDEN: No, I couldn't.

KEN: Give way to the tribal beat, surrender yourself to the music –

> *KEN pulls MRS CORDEN to and gives her a twirl*

MRS CORDEN: Oh, Kenneth.

KEN: Dance.

MRS CORDEN: Whatever will Mr Corden say.

> *They dance*

KEN: He need never know, it's our dark secret.

> *KEN spins her again*

They dance

JOE turns off music

Spoilsport.

The true roots of rock 'n' roll are difficult to discern but it seems beyond question to me that it originates from the primitive beat of tribal Africa unencumbered by the restrictions of civilisation, man as savage, man as beast, a mass of pulsating and contradictory feelings.

MRS CORDEN: People have always loved a jolly black minstrel with a banjo.

KEN: There in lies the difference, the minstrels of rock 'n' roll are white.

MRS CORDEN: What about the poor black ones?

KEN: They just get poorer.

MRS CORDEN: You do know an awful lot about everything Kenneth.

JOE: I have to go.

KEN: We haven't heard your speech.

JOE: I don't have time.

MRS CORDEN: Are you going to thank your mother and father?

JOE: I'm thanking no one, it's my award.

MRS CORDEN: Oh, so that's why you're not going, Kenneth.

KEN: Why go at all, why not let someone else – get Peggy to pick it up for you. What do you need their approval for anyway?

JOE: I don't. I won it, I deserve it.

KEN: You're selling out.

JOE: It's all right for you to talk about selling out, you had something to sell in the first place. I've got nothing, I come from nothing.

KEN: That's the difference between the middle classes and the working class; the middle classes have ideals, visions of utopia, while the working class is all about how to get there, the nuts and bolts, the road map, the aspirations.

JOE: I do, I have to go.

MRS CORDEN: Yes, you do.

JOE: I do.

MRS CORDEN: You don't want to be late.

JOE: No.

MRS CORDEN: I'll take the tea things in the kitchen.

> *Exit MRS CORDEN with teapot*

JOE: I have to pick up Peggy.

KEN: Yes.

> *JOE makes to go*

Wait.

> *Straightens JOE's tie*

There.

JOE: How do I look?

KEN: Dressed to kill.

JOE: Wish me luck.

KEN: You don't need it, you've got more luck than is obscenely allowable for any one man.

JOE: It won't last.

KEN: Oh, no.

Exit JOE

Phone rings
KEN answers

The Orton residence. No I'm afraid he's not. Who shall I say called. Concerning anything in particular. Yes, I see. I will. As soon as he gets in.

Puts down phone

Enter MRS CORDEN

MRS CORDEN: Who was that?

KEN: The Beatles. They want him to write a film script for them.

MRS CORDEN: Is there no end.

KEN: Apparently not.

Exit MRS CORDEN

Enter JOE holding Evening Standard Award.
Spotlight on him frontstage and one on KEN upstage holding a bottle of pills in silence

JOE: I want to thank everyone involved in *Loot*, and the cast in particular, for making this award possible. In the early days we used to give complimentary tickets to various organisations. We sent a few to Scotland Yard. And the police loved the play so much that they rang up asking for more tickets. Everyone else thinks the play's fantasy. Of course the police know that it's true. I hope to get another of these in about two years time, for the other end of the mantelpiece. Thank you.

Applause

JOE places award on desk and exits

Music, Schubert piano Lullaby

KEN takes a tablet

71

Then another

KEN: *Nil desperandum.*

> *Undresses down to underpants*
> *Lies on his bed*

> *Light fades*
> *The music continues*

> *Between this scene and the next some more spaces in the collage*
> *are filled in and the wall becomes more oppressive*

TWO

> *KEN in bed*
> *Night*
> *Listening to the music from above*
> *On the radio*

> *Enter JOE*
> *Turns off radio*
> *JOE sits at desk and switches on light*

KEN: I was listening to that.

JOE: I thought you were asleep.

KEN: I am.

> *KEN switches on his bedside light*

There's a broadcast coming up from Earls Court, an exhibition of caged birds and their owners.

JOE: I know how they feel.

> *JOE begins to write*

KEN: You have an entry to make in your diary.

JOE: I thought you were sleeping.

KEN: I don't sleep.

JOE: Take a tablet.

KEN: I don't want a tablet.

JOE: You got some from the doctor, the doctor gave you some.

KEN: Nembutal.

JOE: That's right, so you can sleep.

KEN: In case of emergencies. Is this an emergency?

JOE: I don't know. Is it?

KEN: Nembutal, it's what Hitler issued in concentrated form to his bunker staff in the eventuality of defeat.

JOE: I always knew you were a facist.

KEN: You've started a diary.

JOE: Peggy said to.

KEN: Oh, Peggy.

JOE: Yes, Peggy.

KEN: And I suppose you'd roll around in the street stark bollock naked smothered in olive oil if Peggy said.

JOE: If I thought there was some advantage to it, yes.

KEN: Marry her why don't you, and stop this charade.

JOE: It's not a charade. She's my agent.

KEN: Cow.

JOE: You like her.

KEN: So. Diabetics like sugar but that doesn't mean they should eat it.

JOE: She helped organise an exhibition of your collages.

KEN: To placate me.

JOE: She got all her friends to come.

KEN: They didn't buy.

JOE: She did.

KEN: Yes. It's a love triangle, you me and Peggy, but the only person getting any sex is you and it's not with either of us. Cow.

JOE: No wonder you haven't got any friends.

KEN: I don't like people.

JOE: What do you say about me behind my back when I'm not here?

KEN: I don't, there's no one to say it to.

JOE: Then go out and meet someone.

KEN: Oh, you'd like that wouldn't you, suit you nicely – justify your inability to keep your cock down your pants once you're out the front door – me meeting someone else, a complete justification for your sexual incontinence.

JOE: So you choose not to, to spite me.

KEN: No, because I don't want to, I only want you.

JOE: Stop whining.

KEN: I'm not.

JOE: You do.

KEN: I don't.

> *Silence*

> *JOE writes*

I read the new draft of *What the Butler Saw.*

JOE: I've given it to Peggy to read.

KEN: I've got one or two notes about the deranged psychiatrist.

> *Silence*

Talk to me.

JOE: I am..

> *Silence*

> *JOE writes*

KEN: Did you meet anyone nice on your way back home.

JOE: I'm not interested in nice.

KEN: Tell me.

JOE: No, if you want sex then go out and get it, you're not having it through me vicariously.

KEN: That's not what I want.

JOE: What do you want?

KEN: You know what I want. Bastard.

JOE: Yes that's right I'm a bastard. I like sex – in dimly lit back rooms, up dark back alleys, on canal tow paths, in public toilets – anywhere with men who are desperate enough to do it – the sheer bloody outrageous indecency of it all – no niceties, no pretence, pure sex – I tell you, if there were more people doing it in the street the whole iniquitous class ridden edifice we call society would crumble. No. I know what I am.

KEN: Bastard.

JOE: Yes.

> *Closes diary*

KEN: Don't let me stop you.

JOE: I'm not.

KEN: What do you need a diary for anyway?

JOE: Posterity.

KEN: I'll bet the only thing posterior about it is all the rear ends in it.

JOE: And there'll be no sissy asterisks in my diary, I'll publish it and be damned.

KEN: What about the truth.

JOE: What truth?

KEN: The truth about me. I know you, you'll write it from your own point of view to make yourself look good.

JOE: It's my diary.

KEN: So, now you've found yet another way to exclude me.

JOE: Exclude you from what?

KEN: Everything. You wouldn't be who you are without me. Look at him, the serious writer. Who was it who taught you to take yourself seriously in the first place? And this is the thanks I get. I give you everything and you give me nothing.

JOE: Then leave.

KEN: It's my flat.

JOE: All right, I'll go.

KEN: I'll kill myself.

JOE: Go on then.

KEN: Then you'll see.

JOE: I'm not excluding you Kenneth, I just think it's bad to live in each other's pockets twenty-four hours a day three hundred and sixty-five days of the year.

KEN: I'll show you.

JOE: Why, what are you going to do?

KEN: I don't know.

JOE: Go out, that'd be a shock.

KEN: Right, I will.

JOE: When?

KEN: Soon.

JOE: Tomorrow?

KEN: Maybe.

JOE: What's stopping you?

KEN: Nothing.

JOE: Then go on, go out on your own.

KEN: I am, I will. On my bike.

JOE: Pump up your tyres.

KEN: Get my pump out.

JOE: Put some air in your tyres.

KEN: Yes, I will.

JOE: I'll come with you.

KEN: You can stay at home and come on your own.

JOE: Right.

KEN: Right.

> *JOE opens diary and writes in it*
>
> *KEN opens bottle of pills and hurriedly takes two*

JOE: That's right, take a tablet.

KEN: What are you writing?

JOE: Nothing.

> *JOE closes his diary and puts it by the typewriter*

It's private.

KEN: I wouldn't want to read about your sordid little life for all the tea in China.

JOE: Good.

Turns out desk light and makes for door

KEN: Where are you going?

JOE: Out.

KEN takes a tablet

That won't save you.

KEN: Firstly, I don't want saving. Secondly, if I did I wouldn't want saving by you, I'd do it myself. And thirdly –

JOE: You couldn't save anyone, not the state you're in.

KEN: Thirdly –

JOE: You're too selfish to think of anyone but yourself.

KEN: I saved you from the boring little life you would have had as a stupid naïve working class boy from Leicester.

JOE: And thirdly.

KEN: I want an apology.

JOE: For what?

KEN: Everything.

JOE: I know what I need and I'm going out to get it.

KEN: Animal.

JOE: Yes, that's what we are. We eat, we breath, we fuck we die, so make the most of it while you can. Consciousness is nature's cruel trick to try and stop us from having fun.

KEN: What are you writing?

JOE: Nothing.

KEN: It's about me.

JOE: It's private.

KEN: How can it be if it's about me?

JOE: Just a few notes.

KEN: Infernal diary.

JOE: I have to go.

KEN: I have a right to see what you've written.

JOE: No you don't.

KEN: Where are you going?

JOE: Out.

KEN: Out where?

JOE: Just out.

KEN: Animal. I'll read it while you're gone.

JOE: You do that.

KEN: I will.

JOE: Yes do.

KEN: I will, I'll read your diary.

JOE: That's what it's for. Medication. Chin, chin.

> *Exit JOE*

KEN: Right.

> *KEN gets out of bed*
> *Turns on desk light*
> *Paces to and fro*

No.

> *Switches off desk light and turns away*

Damn.

> *Turns light on sits and stares at diary*
> *Goes to open it*

No.

> *Turns off light and gets back into bed*

I won't read it. I don't want to read it. His sad little life.

> *Pulls up bedcover turns out light tosses and turns*
> *Turns on light and sits up*

Bugger.

> *Turns on desk light*
> *Sits at desk*
> *Opens diary and reads it*

THREE

> *MRS CORDEN stands looking at the collage wall above JOE's bed*
> *Written across it in big letters is* **JOE ORTON IS A SPINELESS TWAT**
>
> *JOE sitting on the bed in front of her*

MRS CORDEN: (*Reading wall.*) 'Joe Orton is a spineless –'

JOE: 'Twat.'

MRS CORDEN: He's still not back.

JOE: No.

MRS CORDEN: This isn't like Kenneth at all.

JOE: I've never waited up for him, not in fifteen years.

MRS CORDEN: He'll be all right. Still, it's a pity about his wall.

It's his pride and joy. Things are getting difficult.

JOE: No, no, not at all.

MRS CORDEN: When Mr Corden has one of his turns I usually give him a toffee and that normally does the trick.

JOE: If only Kenneth was that easy.

MRS CORDEN: Or in graver circumstances, a pear drop.

JOE: Thanks for the tip.

MRS CORDEN: Don't mention it. I'll worry about you when we're gone, but there's no looking back, not now, not now Mr Corden's retired and we're moving to the country. Mr Corden says I'm not to fret, he doesn't want me upsetting his retirement, but it's like I tell him, a tiger won't change its stripes, not for anyone.

JOE: Oh, we'll be all right.

MRS CORDEN: It's Kenneth I worry about most.

JOE: Don't worry about Ken, he's tough as old boots.

MRS CORDEN: Mr Corden's been looking forward to this all his life. I expect I shall have to get used to him being round the house a bit more.

JOE: Yes, you will.

MRS CORDEN: The company gave him a carriage lamp and an alarm clock, in recognition of his long service record – man and boy all his life, with only a five year break in which to fight for King and country.

JOE: And you've been with him all that time.

MRS CORDEN: In sickness and in health.

JOE: You've never contemplated – I mean, Mr Corden, he's your first, the only one, there's never been anyone else.

MRS CORDEN: As a younger woman you know John I had many admirers, including the now minister of transport's brother.

JOE: But you didn't like him.

MRS CORDEN: He put his hand on my knee under the table in The Golden Egg one day and asked me to runaway to Derby with him, I said no. Derby. The greatest regret of my life.

JOE: You've never thought of leaving?

MRS CORDEN: He couldn't manage without me.

JOE: But if he could, if he could manage without you.

MRS CORDEN: Kenneth's devoted to you.

JOE: That's not a reason for staying with someone is it?

MRS CORDEN: You must do what you have to John.

Enter KEN in wig

The wandering minstrel returns.

KEN: You got my message.

JOE: Loud and clear.

MRS CORDEN: I'll leave you two boys to it.

KEN: Oh, I see, I choose to stay out and I'm in trouble. Is this what it's like when Mr Corden comes home late.

MRS CORDEN: He never does. I wish he would.

KEN: There's a first time for everything.

JOE: Yes, yes there is.

Exit MRS CORDEN

What does this mean.

KEN: Exactly what it says. You and your new spineless friends. They treat me like dirt. They think I'm a no one.

JOE: It's not true is it?

KEN: No.

JOE: You don't believe it, do you?

KEN: Of course not.

JOE: Then forget it.

KEN: And here, take it, take your wig back – you don't want it, I don't want it – it doesn't work, it fell off –

JOE laughs

I don't want to be sucked off in the dark by a dwarf I've never even met before in my life in a public place

JOE: You want an introduction.

KEN: No.

JOE: You want to fall in love and get married.

KEN: Of course not, don't be absurd – yes.

JOE laughs

This isn't funny, it's not funny.

JOE: I know.

KEN: Go on laugh. Like everyone else, everyone out there and everyone in your diary. Who is that wig for anyway. You or me. Your embarrassment. My shame.

KEN picks up Evening Standard Award and throws it at JOE

Give me what I want, or go.

JOE: You want me to go.

KEN: What do you want. You couldn't.

JOE: That's what you want.

KEN: You know what I want.

JOE: No, Kenneth, no I don't.

KEN: You need me to write.

JOE: You need me to breathe.

KEN: Go on then go.

JOE: Here –

> *JOE picks up KEN's bottle of tablets*

Take a tablet why don't you.

KEN: I don't want one.

JOE: Look, you've got all sorts of colours here, all mixed up together in one big bottle – purple ones, yellow ones, red ones, white ones too – which one do you want, or just any at random –

> *Grabs KEN's hand*

Blindfold –

KEN: Let go.

JOE: Stick your hand in and see what you get.

KEN: Let go of my hand.

JOE: Have a tablet.

KEN: I don't want a tablet.

JOE: You need a tablet, that's why you've got them – they calm you down.

KEN: I don't want calming down. Let go will you.

> *KEN pulls away*

JOE: You need to calm down.

KEN: I am calm, I'm calm, don't tell me to calm down.

> *JOE taunts KEN with bottle*

JOE: You haven't taken your tablet.

KEN: I don't want a tablet.

JOE: Calm, calm.

KEN: I'm calm all right –

Picks up chair

I'm calm.

Smashes chair on floor

Right.

JOE: Right.

KEN sits on bed and puts his head in his hands

Enter MRS CORDEN

MRS CORDEN: I heard banging. Everything's all right?

JOE: It's all right.

MRS CORDEN: Everything's all all right.
You're sure?

JOE: Yes.

MRS CORDEN: You don't want me to stop.

JOE: No it's all right.

MRS CORDEN: You don't want to go out.

JOE: No, I'll stop. I've decided to stop.

MRS CORDEN: If you change your mind.

JOE: No, I won't. I'm stopping.

MRS CORDEN: You're sure.

JOE: I'm sure.

MRS CORDEN: You know where I am.

JOE: Yes, yes thank you.

Exit MRS CORDEN

JOE takes out a new suitcase from under his bed

Puts it on the bed

KEN: You're going.

Silence

You've even bought a new suitcase for the occasion.

Silence

You've been planning this for months.

JOE: Look under your bed.

KEN: Why, what venomous trap have you set for me there.

JOE: Just look.

KEN pulls out a suitcase from under his bed

We're going to Tangiers.

KEN: Together.

JOE: You'd like to go separately. The Beatles didn't buy the film script, so I decided this was a good time to go. You like Tangiers. Lets pack.

JOE puts on record, 'You Mustn't Kick it Around', Pal Joey

KEN opens his suitcase and packs

JOE exits into bathroom

KEN: Things are always so much better in Tangiers, over there we're anonymous, over there nobody cares about Joe Orton, over there there's no one to interfere with us.

Enter JOE with two toothbrushes

JOE: Just plenty of Arab boys for us to interfere with.

JOE gives toothbrush to KEN

KEN throws it in his suitcase
Shuts the lid tight and picks it up

KEN: Sun, sand, sex, money and boys.

JOE: Tangiers. It's our country.

JOE picks up his suitcase
Exit JOE and KEN

Between the end of this scene and the next the final white spaces
on the collage fill in and the wall is complete. Oppressive and
dark

FOUR

Suitcases open on both beds and contents strewn everywhere
KEN in pyjamas
Mending broken chair with hammer and nails
Listening to Pal Joey.
Carefully lines up nail
Strikes with hammer
Misses and hits thumb

KEN: Arrrgh!

Opens bottle of tablets and takes a couple
Turns off music

Damn chair.

Sits on bed
Looks to where diary is

No. No. No.

Picks up telephone and dials

KEN: Hello, hello – yes, yes it's Kenneth – fine, fine – we got
back a month ago – John's been up in Leicester but he's
back now. Out. Yes, we're fine. How are you? And Mr
Corden? Good, good.

Silence

Well, I just wanted to say hello, see you're all right since
you moved. I will. I will. And say hello to Mr Corden.

Puts phone down

Looks at diary

No.

Picks up phone and dials

Hello. Is that the Samaritans. No, no I don't want to talk. Well, if you really cared you'd have rung me.

Puts phone down
KEN opens bottle of tablets tips them in a pile on the floor and separates out four by colour

One purple, one red, one yellow, one white –

Then methodically counts out another four tablets
Checking them off by colour as he goes

One purple, one red, one yellow, one white –

Phone rings
KEN stops
Looks at phone
Picks up receiver

Hello. Yes earlier. No. It's fine. Really I'm fine doctor. I don't need emergency help. It can wait till tomorrow. I'll see you tomorrow. John will be back soon. Thank you for calling.

Puts phone down

Goes back to counting tablets

Purple, red, yellow, white –

Stops
Pauses

No.

Shovels them back in bottle and screws the top back on

There.

Turns on music: Pal Joey.

Paces
Changes record track
Paces
Turns off music

Damn chair.

Kicks chair

Arrrgh!

Hops to bed and sits on it nursing his foot

Bloody chair, bloody diary, bloody Joe Orton – sod it.

Picks up JOE's diary
Sits before tape recorder
Switches it on
Theme tune to Mrs Dale's Diary

The diary of Joe Orton, a Somebody – a recording of the daily happenings in his life – of an everyday talentless mediocre second rate opportunistic playwright twat.

Opens the diary at well thumbed page
Presses 'record' button

(*KEN reads aloud parodying the voices of JOE, Peter Willes and himself.*) 'Went to Peter Willes's for dinner. When we got there he stared at Kenneth in horror – 'That's an old Etonian tie!' he screeched. 'Yes,' Kenneth said. 'It's a joke'. You're making people angry,' Willes said. 'I don't care,' Kenneth said, laughing a little too readily.

KEN does so

'I want to make them angry.' 'But why?' Willes said. 'People dislike you enough already, why make them more angry? It's permissible as a foible of youth, but you – ' (*Pauses.*) 'But you – a middle-aged nonentity – it's sad and pathetic.'

KEN looks up from diary
Turns off tape recorder

Enter JOE

KEN snaps diary shut, turns off tape recorder, shovels tablets back in bottle and screws on top

JOE: What are you doing?

KEN: Mending the chair.

JOE throws off coat

JOE: Stop reading my diary, it only makes you more miserable than you already are.

KEN: I've always been of the opinion that it's better to be included and tortured than left out and ignored.

JOE: You've turned out to be a real nag.

KEN: If only we could get away from all this.

JOE: I don't suppose you've been out today have you?

KEN: No.

JOE: Not even the shops.

KEN: We've got all we need.

JOE: So, what have you been doing all day – stood in front of the mirror admiring yourself.

KEN: I've been standing at the sink, washing your fucking underpants.

JOE: All right, all right.

KEN: We should, get right away. Somewhere by the sea, a desert island where there is no one, just you me, endless copulation and death.

JOE: You'd get bored.

KEN: You'd get bored.

JOE: I'd be all right.

KEN: Yes, you'll make do with anything – animal, vegetable or mineral, as long as there's an opening. But we could, now that you've got a bit of money, we could get somewhere bigger, less central.

JOE: There isn't anywhere.

KEN: Croydon.

JOE: I'm not going to Croydon.

KEN: You've never been.

JOE: I don't want to. I'm serious Kenneth, I'm not living in Croydon.

KEN: You've no sense of adventure.

JOE: Tight arsed suburbanite.

KEN: Guttersnipe.

JOE: That's right, I'm from the gutter.

KEN: And who was it that raised you, like Lazarus from the dead.

JOE: So now you're the son of God.

KEN: Type cast again.

JOE: Yes, I'm from the gutter, and don't you forget it.

KEN: Fat chance, you only have to get whiff of a journalist in the room and you're up on your cross, a crucified working class tart bleeding all over the carpet showing off her stigmata.

JOE: We're not moving to Croydon.

KEN: I'm not suggesting castration.

JOE: We move to Croydon you might as well. Chop off both our balls, have them pickled in a jar and stood on the mantelpiece, that or nail them to the wall like flying ducks.

KEN: Croydon's not fixed.

JOE: Don't.

KEN: How about East Grinstead.

JOE: I said, no.

KEN: Why not, somebody's got to live there.

JOE: The dead.

KEN: That can be arranged.

JOE: Another empty threat.

KEN: You'll see.

JOE: You haven't got it in you.

KEN: No, that's right I don't – the world and his father, anywhere from here to the Holloway Road, any man but me.

JOE: And his son.

KEN: You'll get your just deserts, you'll see.

JOE: I should be so lucky.

KEN: Loveless, Godless, filth and promiscuity – all this homosexuality, it disgusts me.

JOE: I'm not even going to try and unpack that one.

KEN: Unpack, unpack – you've been reading one of those books again.

JOE: Engage with the enemy. You should have seen them at the theatre tonight, rolling in the aisles.

JOE starts to undress

The cast said you'd been in while I was away telling them about our new play *What The Butler Saw.*

KEN: I helped.

JOE: You came up with the title.

KEN: And some of the plot.

JOE: You're good at titles, I do the writing.

KEN: And now you're going to bed.

JOE: I'm tired.

KEN: You're always tired.

JOE: You're never tired.

KEN: I don't sleep.

JOE: And because you don't I can't.

KEN: You only have to put your head on the pillow and you're out like a light.

> *JOE gets into bed leaving his clothes in a pile on the floor*

Slut.

JOE: Leave them.

KEN: I don't and they stay there all night.

JOE: So let them. I don't need you cleaning up after me.

KEN: You walk all over me.

JOE: You let your self be walked on.

KEN: What would you do if I was dead?

JOE: But you're not, now let me sleep.

KEN: You won't listen.

JOE: I listen.

KEN: You don't listen.

JOE: You don't listen.

KEN: You never listen.

JOE: I listen, I'm listening now – you've got something to say, say it or let me sleep. Well.

KEN: You...

JOE: What?

KEN: You're...

JOE: It's always the same. You never say anything.

KEN: I talk –

JOE: I'm listening.

KEN: What, what do you want me to do, you want me to humiliate myself.

JOE: I've got a car coming early to take me to Twickenham Studios, I need to sleep.

KEN picks up scissors

KEN: I'll stab myself, you want that, in the neck – is that what you want, you want me to kill myself so that you can be happy.

JOE: Put down the scissors Kenneth.

KEN: I will, I'll stab myself.

JOE: Just put down the scissors.

KEN: I'll kill myself.

JOE: Stop being hysterical.

KEN: I'm not hysterical.

JOE: I'll call the police.

KEN: Go on then, do that, call them. You do that and I'll tell them about the mental torture.

JOE: What mental torture.

KEN: I've got you worried.

JOE: Yes, I'm worried.

KEN: What are you worried about.

JOE: Put down the scissors Kenneth and I'll tell you.

KEN: What do you know…every day, the supreme effort, one second to the next – the struggle between annihilation and survival, existence and inexistence.

JOE: Give me the scissors.

> *KEN gives scissors to JOE*

Now, go to bed.

> *JOE gets into bed*

KEN: (*Shouts.*) They treat me like shit. You let them treat me like shit. I won't be treated like shit.

JOE: I'm trying to sleep.

KEN: I should kill you.

JOE: Well do it then, do it and then we can all get some sleep. No. Goodnight then.

KEN: You can't be trusted. I need help.

JOE: Ring the Samaritans.

KEN: I'll end up like my father with my head in the oven.

JOE: Not our oven you won't, it's electric.

KEN: Please, help me.

JOE: Go to sleep.

> *JOE turns out bedside light*

KEN: Good night to you as well.

> *KEN turns out bedside light*
>
> *Darkness*

Silence

KEN turns on bedside light

Tell me a story. I can't sleep. Make me sleep. Talk to me.

KEN turns on bedside light

Silence

Talk to me.

JOE: I won't tell you again, turn out your light and go to sleep. Do it Kenneth, or I'm out the door.

KEN: I'd kill you first. All you think you have to do is smile, flash those big dark deep beautiful eyes of yours and that it will all be all right – well it isn't, it's not, it isn't all all right, not any more.

JOE sits up and puts his light on

JOE: Stop your moaning.

Silence

Now take a tablet, go to sleep, and stop acting like a middle-aged non-entity.

KEN: Right.

JOE: Right.

JOE turns light out
KEN turns out light

Darkness

KEN: Right.

KEN gets out of bed
Picks up hammer
And crosses to JOE's bed
The dull thud of nine frenzied hammer blows

KEN turns on light

Wall, bed, JOE and KEN covered with blood

Right. All right. Right.

KEN lays hammer on JOE's bloodied bedspread
KEN takes off his bloody pyjama top stands at typewriter
Inserts fresh piece of paper and types a note
Studies note for a few seconds and then reads it out loud back
to himself

'If you read his diary all will
be explained.
KH
PS. Especially the latter part'

Places note on top of diary
Puts on record
'The flower garden of my heart', Pal Joey
Places bottle of tablets centre stage
Takes tin of grapefruit juice
From bedside
Sits centre stage
Opens the grapefruit juice
Opens bottle of tablets and tips them out
Takes a tablet and washes it down with a swig of juice
Takes a tablet and washes it down with a swig of juice
Takes a tablet and washes it down with a swig of juice
Takes a tablet and washes it down with a swig of grapefruit
juice
He continues to do so

The lights gradually die down
To blackout

The End

NOTES

1) Wireless broadcast for Act One, scene i.

WIRELESS: Finally, the new style pedestrian crossing has been causing confusion and chaos in the capital city. The Panda crossing, described earlier this month by the Minister of Transport Ernest Marples as 'A new idea in pedestrian safety', has so far caused little more than traffic jams, hot tempers and at least one sprained ankle according to the Metropolitan police. One old lady, not impressed, said, 'That man Marples is up to too many tricks. It's a hairbrained scheme and most dangerous'. A spokesman for the AA said, 'It will obviously take some time before drivers and pedestrians understand these new crossings properly.' And now, *Mrs Dale's Diary…*

If used this should be cut to suit the pace of the action and be barely audible.

JOE turns up the volume for the theme tune to Mrs Dale's Diary.

www.ingramcontent.com/pod-product-compliance
Ingram Content Group UK Ltd.
Pitfield, Milton Keynes, MK11 3LW, UK
UKHW020723280225
455688UK00012B/486